LEGO

DC COMICS SUPER HEROES

DEFENDER OF GOTHAM CITY

WRITTEN BY SIMON HUGO AND CAVAN SCOTT

BATMAN CREATED BY BOB KANE WITH BILL FINGER

INTRODUCTION

Batman has taken on many exciting missions. Whether in the sky, underwater, or even in space, the Caped Crusader's devotion to crime-fighting knows no limits.

HOW TO USE THIS BOOK

This book is a guide to some of the coolest LEGO® Batman™ minifigures and vehicles. These amazing minifigures are ordered chronologically according to when they were first released.

CONTENTS

BATMOBILE
WHEN SPEED'S THE NEED

VITAL STATS

OWNER: Batman
USED FOR: Racing and chasing
GEAR: Hidden rockets

SET NAME: Batman: The Riddler Chase
SET NUMBER: 76012
YEAR: 2014

Adjustable rear wing for speed and defence

Twin exhausts

Downward-facing steering wheel

Bargeboards assist airflow for greater speed

POCKET ROCKETS

The back of the Batmobile has a hidden weapon. The entire rear section rises up above the cockpit to become a cannon ready to fire a pair of rockets!

DID YOU KNOW?

This Batmobile is inspired by the one that appears in the *Beware the Batman* animated series.

With its low, broad body and big, wide wheels, this Batmobile looks like a Formula 1 racing car. No wonder Batman uses it to keep up with his speedy Super Hero friend, The Flash – and with the villainous Riddler's own racing dragster.

BATMAN
BEWARE THIS BATMAN

VITAL STATS
....

LIKES: His new Batmobile
DISLIKES: Bombing along
the road
FRIENDS: The Flash
FOES: The Riddler
SKILLS: Racing
GEAR: Batarang

SET NAME: Batman:
The Riddler Chase
SET NUMBER: 76012
YEAR: 2014

DID YOU KNOW?
This outfit is based on
the 2013 animated
series Beware the
Batman, complete with
the show's distinctive
bat-symbol.

Costume
printing
continues on
the back

New style
bat-symbol

New high-tech,
bronzed Utility Belt
has curvier edges
than before.

FACING HIS ENEMIES
Batman may have a sleek new
suit to go with a new Batmobile,
but this minifigure still shares
Batman's standard two-sided
head from earlier variants, plus,
of course, the trusty Batarang.

Grey gloves

Batman debuted a refined look as
well as a new set of wheels when he
had to take to the streets in a race
against the Riddler. Time to buckle
up with that shiny new Utility Belt
and hit the road in the Batmobile!

BATMAN
EARLY KNIGHT

VITAL STATS
....

LIKES: Helping young builders
DISLIKES: Complicated instructions
FRIENDS: Robin
FOES: The Joker
SKILLS: Driving
GEAR: Batarang

SET NAMES: Batman Classic TV Series *Batmobile*, Batman: Defend the Batcave
SET NUMBERS: SDCC037, 10672
YEAR: 2014

A new light blue cowl covers Batman's two-sided head.

Similar body print to the 2012 Batman minifigure

Exclusive bright blue cape only found on this Batman minifigure

TO THE BATCAVE...
Also starring as a San Diego Comic-Con exclusive, this Batman prefers the home comforts of his LEGO® Juniors Batcave in set 10672. However, he needs to fight off the Joker before he can rest easy again...

Available with a LEGO Juniors set, this Batman opts for a friendly bright blue and grey costume. Sticking with a simple theme, he wears a streamlined Utility Belt and a classic yellow bat-symbol.

BATMOBILE
RETRO ROCKET CAR

VITAL STATS
....

OWNER: Batman
USED FOR: Crusading capers
GEAR: On-board computer

SET NAME: Batman Classic
TV Series *Batmobile*
SET NUMBER: SDCC037
YEAR: 2014

Two front
windshields

Light warns
other road users
to clear the way

Aerials transmit calls
to the Batphone

Groovy red trim

RARE RELEASE
This rare set was available only
at the 2014 San Diego Comic-
Con event. It came with Batman
and Robin minifigures, and was
released to mark 75 years of
Batman's adventures.

DID YOU KNOW?
This set is based on
the Batmobile from
the 1960s *Batman*
TV series.

This unusual-looking Batmobile
has a separate seating compartment
for both Batman and Robin. Powered
by atomic batteries, it has a turbo-
boosting rocket at the rear that
blasts a jet of flame. Lucky there's a
bright red warning light on the top!

BATWING
A WING AND A SNARE

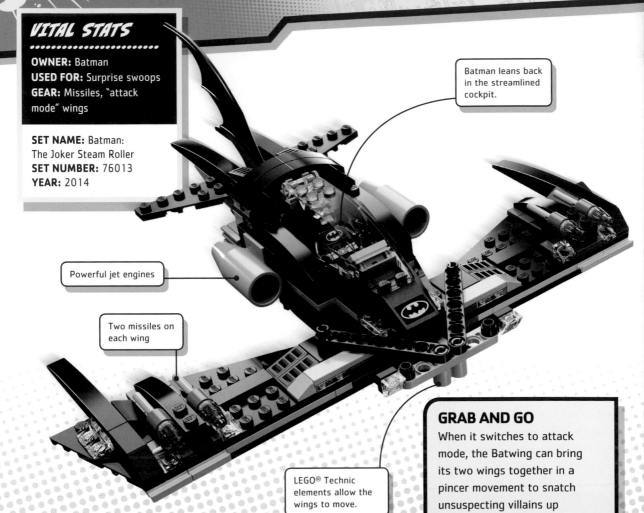

VITAL STATS

OWNER: Batman
USED FOR: Surprise swoops
GEAR: Missiles, "attack mode" wings

SET NAME: Batman: The Joker Steam Roller
SET NUMBER: 76013
YEAR: 2014

Batman leans back in the streamlined cockpit.

Powerful jet engines

Two missiles on each wing

LEGO® Technic elements allow the wings to move.

GRAB AND GO

When it switches to attack mode, the Batwing can bring its two wings together in a pincer movement to snatch unsuspecting villains up from the ground below!

Every bat needs wings, even Batman! This very special Batwing is equipped with four missiles and a surprise attack mode. It's the perfect choice to gain the advantage of height when the Joker takes to the streets with his Steam Roller.

BATMAN
DARK KNIGHT RISING

VITAL STATS

LIKES: Armoured vehicles
DISLIKES: Panic in the streets
FRIENDS: Jim Gordon
FOES: The Joker
SKILLS: Driving
GEAR: Batarang

SET NAME: The Tumbler
SET NUMBER: 76023
YEAR: 2014

Exclusive two-sided face not found on another Batman minifigure.

Unique, beefed-up armour

DID YOU KNOW?

This minifigure is based on the costume worn by Batman in the movie *Batman Begins* and the first half of *The Dark Knight*.

Bronze Utility Belt

READY TO TUMBLE

The other side of this minifigure's double-sided head shows a calm, considerate expression. Batman won't remain calm when he takes the Tumbler out on Gotham City's streets.

It's the Darkest Knight of all. After hanging up the cape and cowl, Bruce comes out of retirement as Batman. Gotham City is more dangerous than ever, meaning that his Batsuit is now more body armour than costume.

TUMBLER
ULTIMATE CRIME FIGHTER'S SERIES

VITAL STATS
....

OWNER: Batman
USED FOR: Looking cool
GEAR: Super-fast jet engine

SET NAME: The Tumbler
SET NUMBER: 76023
YEAR: 2014

Entry/exit by top hatch

Six flaps add drag for sudden stops

DID YOU KNOW?
This Ultimate Collector's Series set is the largest LEGO® DC Comics Super Heroes set to date, with 1,869 pieces.

These front tyres are not found in any other set.

Lights used when not in stealth mode

Hydraulic rods deploy attack mode

COMPLETE CONTROLS
Two panels lift off the roof of the Tumbler to reveal an incredibly detailed cockpit, with two control panels, several display screens, steering controls and a moving LEGO gear lever.

This feat of engineering takes Batman's car collection to a whole new scale! Its huge tyres provide traction, while its angular armour seems to go on forever. At the back, 1,500 horsepower blasts out via a giant jet turbine engine.

SPACE BATMAN
COSMIC CAPED CRUSADER

VITAL STATS

LIKES: Exploring
DISLIKES: Extra-terrestrial thieves
FRIENDS: Green Lantern
FOES: Sinestro
SKILLS: Space flight
GEAR: Extending wings

SET NAME: Green Lantern vs Sinestro
SET NUMBER: 76025
YEAR: 2015

Silver cowl with shorter ears

Wings in closed formation

Air tubes for breathing in space

Space suit printed on both sides of body

Silver arms and legs

SPACE FLIGHT

The Space Batman variant comes with two translucent plastic capes. Remove Batman's rocket pack to switch over to the outstretched bat-wings and take flight after Sinestro.

In space, two heads are better than one. The first is printed with a special visor and breathing apparatus, while this Cosmic Caped Crusader variant also comes with a separate, standard two-sided head.

BATMAN
NEW KNIGHT

VITAL STATS

LIKES: New technology
DISLIKES: Low morals
FRIENDS: Wonder Woman,
The Flash
FOES: Gorilla Grodd,
Captain Cold
SKILLS: Piloting his Bat-Mech
GEAR: Batarang

SET NAMES: Gorilla Grodd
Goes Bananas, Batboat
Harbour Pursuit
SET NUMBERS: 76026,
76034
YEAR: 2015

Cape made from new
fabric material

Body armour
with larger black
bat-symbol

New chinless black
cowl similar to
Batman's space
suit helmet

Two-sided head

BOOT-LEGGER BATMAN

The Batman minifigure from
Jokerland (set 76035) is the
only variant to feature a pair
of boots. Complete with a dark
grey suit and golden Utility Belt,
he is ready to take the Gotham
City underworld by storm!

Like Wonder Woman, this Batman
minifigure is based on new costume
designs first introduced to the
comics in 2011. Batman now wears
detailed body armour printed on the
front and back of the minifigure.

BAT·MECH
DESTINED FOR BIG THINGS

Batman at
the controls

Wing
armour

Arms can
move in all
directions

Net-shooter arm

Twin stud
shooters

Broad
feet for
balance

A rare
LEGO
thumb!

NET-WORKING

Batman can catch criminals with
one hand using his Bat-Mech!
The vehicle's right hand is a
cannon containing a net that
flies out to ensnare villains at
the touch of a button. On this
occasion, The Flash came along
to help rope up Grodd, too.

Batman designed this Bat-Mech
for one-on-one combat with giant-
sized bad guys like Gorilla Grodd.
Its multi-jointed arms and legs are a
match for the most flexible of foes,
and its size and strength makes it
one of the city's real big-hitters!

BATMAN
BACK UNDERWATER

Uses a similar double-sided head to the previous Scuba minifigure

A newer softer cape

TEST DIVE
Even though Black Manta abducting the Boy Wonder is annoying, it does give Batman a chance to test the brand new Bat Sub. Not all bad, then!

With the same body as the Jokerland Batman, this deep-sea Detective also uses a revised cowl. The new helmet doesn't include a chin guard, so there's printing of the mask on Batman's head itself.

BAT SUB
DOUBLE DIVER

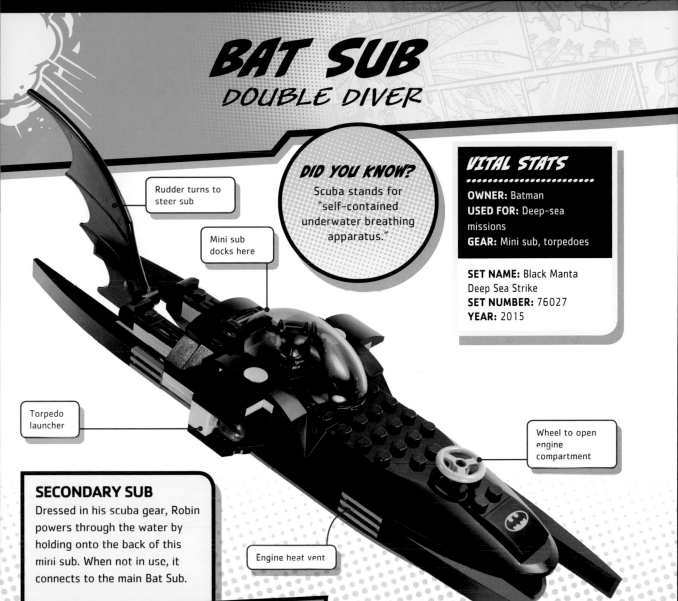

Rudder turns to
steer sub

Mini sub
docks here

DID YOU KNOW?
Scuba stands for
"self-contained
underwater breathing
apparatus."

VITAL STATS
....

OWNER: Batman
USED FOR: Deep-sea
missions
GEAR: Mini sub, torpedoes

SET NAME: Black Manta
Deep Sea Strike
SET NUMBER: 76027
YEAR: 2015

Torpedo
launcher

Wheel to open
engine
compartment

Engine heat vent

SECONDARY SUB

Dressed in his scuba gear, Robin
powers through the water by
holding onto the back of this
mini sub. When not in use, it
connects to the main Bat Sub.

More like a shark than a bat, this
long, slim sub slices through water
at high speed, in search of its prey:
the villainous Black Manta! It is
actually two underwater vehicles in
one, with a small, detachable glider
docked at the back.

BATBOAT
BATMAN'S CATAMARAN

Radar tower lies flat at high speeds

Empty missile launcher

Levers release hovercraft from main section

VITAL STATS
....

OWNER: Batman
USED FOR: Aquatic adventures
GEAR: Missiles, blasters, radar tower

SET NAME: The Batboat Harbour Pursuit
SET NUMBER: 76034
YEAR: 2015

TOWER OF POWER

The tall radar tower lifts up to reveal a bank of high-tech control screens where Robin can track enemy vessels. But beware – there's a trapdoor hidden underneath!

Front blasters detach with cockpits

Each cockpit has its own controls

Batman and Robin are full-steam ahead in this double-hulled Batboat! Its cockpits can split off to become two hovercraft armed with blasters. The remaining control centre runs on autopilot with a retractable radar tower defended by missiles.

BATMOBILE
HEROIC HOT ROD

Jet turbine

Rear weaponry

Detachable cockpit canopy

Turbocharger

DOUBLE DEFENCE
The Batmobile is armed from end to end, with two spring-loaded missiles hidden in the front turbine and two stud shooters beneath the wings at the back.

This Batmobile is one huge jet engine, with a big round turbine drawing in air at the front and a turbocharger adding extra power at the back. The roof lifts right off so Batman can leap into action at top speed, too!

BATCYCLE
LONGER, WIDER, STRONGER

VITAL STATS
....

OWNER: Batman
USED FOR: Narrow escapes
GEAR: Grapple, shooters

SET NAMES: Batman: Gotham City Cycle Chase
SET NUMBERS: 76053
YEARS: 2016

Afterburner glows with heat

Silver Batarang stored at the back

Bat-symbol on fuel tank

ARMED ARMS
Backward-facing shooters on both sides of the rear wheel can flip round and fire to the front or sides. The right-hand arm also has a grapple gun and the left holds a Batarang.

Laser cannons in front lights

Batman's motorcycle has wheels as wide as he is! The Caped Crusader keeps a low profile between the monster-truck tyres and dual shooters can target enemies tearing away in front of the bike or giving chase behind it.

ARMOURED BATMAN
GLOWERS IN THE DARK

VITAL STATS
....

LIKES: Saving the world
DISLIKES: Mysterious aliens
FRIENDS: Alfred
FOES: Superman
SKILLS: Armoured combat
GEAR: Bazooka, grapple,
Batarang

SET NAMES: Clash of
the Heroes
SET NUMBERS: 76044
YEARS: 2016

Glow-in-the-
dark eyes

Chunky
armour
covers
torso

Silver Batarang
fixes on back

BAZOOKA BUILD

Batman's three-in-one weapon
can be built as a stud-shooting
bazooka with two handles, or as
a smaller stud-shooter and a
separate grapple launcher for
Batman to hold in each hand.

Sometimes, even Super Heroes
squabble – and when Batman takes
on Superman in a rooftop duel, he'll
need his most impressive armour!
This combat suit has grips to store
equipment and protective plating.

BATWING
FLYING ALL THROUGH THE NIGHT

VITAL STATS

OWNER: Batman
USED FOR: Chasing Lex Luthor
GEAR: Rapid-fire shooter

SET NAMES: Heroes of Justice: Sky-High Battle
SET NUMBERS: 76046
YEARS: 2016

Cockpit opens in two sections

DID YOU KNOW?
The Batwing's rotating cannon has six rapid-fire launchers. Lex Luthor, in his helicopter, needs to watch out!

Small silver bat-symbol on cannon

WINGING IT

In flight, the Batwing gains lift by extending its wings in a "V" formation. In landing mode, its wings retract and its fins fold up to create a smaller and squarer silhouette.

Wings fully extended for flight mode

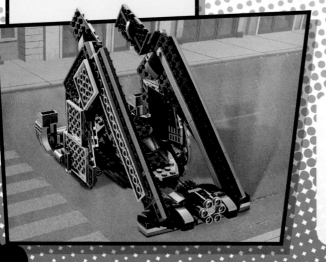

When Superman is on the scene, Batman needs wings to keep up with the action! The Caped Crusader jumps into this stealth flyer to join the Last Son of Krypton in pursuit of Lex Luthor.

BATMOBILE
CARRIAGE OF JUSTICE

VITAL STATS

OWNER: Batman
USED FOR: Getting around Gotham City
GEAR: Front and side cannons

SET NAMES: Kryptonite Interception
SET NUMBERS: 76045
YEARS: 2016

Cockpit opens in two sections

Armoured plates protect rear wheels

Stud shooters at front

Recessed front lights

FORK IN THE ROAD
A forklift truck might seem like no match for the Batmobile, but this LexCorp model is armed with flick missiles and driven by a henchman with a stud-shooting bazooka!

Ideal for a trip to Metropolis, this Batmobile is heavily armed and armoured against superpowered attack. Silver details include side vents and a shield-like bat-symbol on the hood, plus shiny shooters to bring a touch of bling to any battle!

BATMAN
BACK WITH A "BAM!"

VITAL STATS

LIKES: Law-abiding citizens
DISLIKES: Dastardly traps
FRIENDS: Robin, Alfred
FOES: Catwoman, the Joker, the Penguin, the Riddler
SKILLS: Science, maths, grammar
GEAR: Batarang

SET NAMES: *Batman* Classic TV Series – Batcave
SET NUMBERS: 76052
YEARS: 2016

Cowl with printed frown

Physique shows through tight suit

TRUE OR FALSE?

Batman has all sorts of high-tech equipment in his Batcave laboratory, including a huge atomic reactor, radar screens and a lie detector with green and red lights on top.

Trusty Batarang

Batman is a brilliant inventor and his unique Utility Belt is full of gadgets for every occasion. He has even invented a dance called the "Batusi." It helps him keep in shape for his never-ending battle against the rogues of Gotham City!

BRUCE WAYNE
THE MAN BEHIND THE MASK

Neat, no-nonsense hair

Stylish cravat in open shirt

Wayne family crest on blazer

DID YOU KNOW?
The classic *Batman* TV series ran for three seasons between 1966 and 1968, with a total of 120 episodes!

RED ALERT
As well as being filled with all his sporting trophies, Bruce's study is also home to a bright red telephone. This gives the Gotham City police a direct line to Batman and Robin.

The billionaire owner of Wayne Manor is accomplished at riding horseback, fishing, climbing and marbles. He gives money to charity and cares for his young ward, Dick Grayson. On top of that, he has a sharp suit – and he's also Batman!

BATMOBILE
WELL-EQUIPPED WHEELS

VITAL STATS
....

OWNER: Batman
USED FOR: Foiling diabolical schemes
GEAR: Shooters, grapples

SET NAMES: *Batman* Classic TV Series – Batcave
SET NUMBERS: 76052
YEARS: 2016

Batphone hidden between seats

Dual exhaust pipes

Bazookas for blasting through walls

GRAPPLES AND PAIRS
The trunk of the Batmobile opens to reveal enough room for two grappling hooks and ropes for scaling the sides of buildings, three Batarangs and a pair of handcuffs.

Pow! Blasting out from the Batcave beneath stately Wayne Manor, this gadget-packed Batmobile is the coolest car of the 1960s. Gotham City was pretty different back then, but the Dynamic Duo never go out of fashion!

BATCOPTER
EARLY WHIRLYBIRD

Wings cast a shadow to scare crooks

VITAL STATS
....

OWNER: Batman
USED FOR: Search and rescue missions
GEAR: Missiles

SET NAMES: *Batman* Classic TV Series – Batcave
SET NUMBERS: 76052
YEARS: 2016

Domed cockpit for an all-round view

MADE FOR TWO

The Boy Wonder takes another seat in the sidecar of this two-person Batcycle. It has space for a handy spare tyre and is also part of the *Batman* Classic TV Series Batcave set.

Missile in flight

Robin takes the controls of this classic 'copter, which dates from the same time and communicates on the same channel as the Batmobile on p.7. It has wings to aid its flight and shark-repelling missiles for missions at sea!

PIRATE BATMAN
BOOK BUCCANEER

VITAL STATS
....

LIKES: Buried treasure
DISLIKES: Walking the plank
FRIENDS: The sea
FOES: Brainiac
SKILLS: Swashbuckling
GEAR: Flail, cutlass

SET NAMES: DK's LEGO *DC Comics Character Encyclopedia*
YEARS: 2016

DID YOU KNOW?
This exclusive minifigure is only available with the trade edition of DK's LEGO *DC Comics Super Heroes Character Encyclopedia.*

No other Batman minifigure wears this chinless cowl in blue.

Spiked flail for self-defence

Utility Belt worn across chest

BACK THROUGH TIME
Pirate Batman is the only LEGO version so far to feature a bat-symbol on the back of his torso (though it is partly hidden by his piratical Utility Belt).

Curved sword called a cutlass

Shiver me timbers – Batman's a buccaneer! Thrown back in time by Brainiac's Time Ray, this Dark Knight dresses as a pirate to fit in with the seafarers he finds himself amongst. He must rescue Green Lantern before returning to the present day!

MIGHTY MICROS: BATMAN
DIMINUTIVE DARK KNIGHT

VITAL STATS

LIKES: Microscopes
DISLIKES: Micromanagement
FRIENDS: Mighty Micros:
Robin
FOES: Mighty Micros:
Catwoman
SKILLS: Making short work
of villains
GEAR: Batarang

SET NAMES: Mighty Micros:
Batman vs Catwoman
SET NUMBERS: 76061
YEARS: 2016

Determined jaw
under chinless cowl

Utility Belt
holds up mini
trousers

Cape flows down
to the ground

MIGHTY
MiCROS

Scaled-up bat-symbol
fits with wackier
Mighty Micros universe

CARTON CAPERS

Batman can snatch stolen milk
from Catwoman's claws in his
Mighty Micros Batmobile. With
a super-speedy afterburner, it's
just the thing for a dairy derby!

The first ever Batman with mini
legs isn't short on crimefighting
skills! He still represents the long
arm of the law, and his cape seems
extra large by comparison. He is
the only Batman minifigure with
different coloured legs and torso.

 Penguin Random House

Project Editor Emma Grange
Editors Tina Jindal, Matt Jones, Ellie Barton,
Clare Millar, Rosie Peet
Senior Designers Nathan Martin, Mark Penfound,
David McDonald
Designers Karan Chaudhary, Stefan Georgiou
Pre-Production Producer Kavita Varma
Senior Producer Lloyd Robertson
Managing Editors Paula Regan,
Chitra Subramanyam
Design Managers Neha Ahuja, Guy Harvey
Creative Manager Sarah Harland
Art Director Lisa Lanzarini
Publisher Julie Ferris
Publishing Director Simon Beecroft

Additional Photography Markos Chouris,
Christopher Chouris, Gary Ombler

First published in Great Britain in 2016
by Dorling Kindersley Limited
80 Strand, London, WC2R 0RL

001–298875–Jul/16

Contains content previously published in LEGO® DC COMICS
SUPER HEROES *Character Encyclopedia* (2016)

Page design copyright © 2016 Dorling Kindersley Limited
A Penguin Random House Company

A CIP catalogue record for this book
is available from the British Library.

ISBN: 978-0-2412-9285-3

Printed and bound in China

www.LEGO.com
www.dk.com
A WORLD OF IDEAS:
SEE ALL THERE IS TO KNOW

ACKNOWLEDGEMENTS

DK would like to thank Randi Sørensen,
Paul Hansford, Martin Leighton Lindhardt, Maria
Bloksgaard Markussen, Adam Corbally, Daniel
Mckenna, Casper Glahder, Adam Siegmund Grabowski,
John Cuppage, Justin Ramsden, Karl Oskar Jonas
Norlen, Marcos Bessa, Sally Aston, Sven Robin Kahl
and Mauricio Bedolla at the LEGO Group; Ben Harper,
Thomas Zellers and Melanie Swartz at Warner Bros.;
Cavan Scott and Simon Hugo for their writing;
Katie Bowden for editorial assistance and Sam
Bartlett for design assistance.